# Positive Poe

MW01485579

## —to encourage your times

James Scott Bernard

Bernard Publishing

Warrenton, Oregon 97146

ISBN 978-0-9961665-6-0

This book is meant to be an encouragement to you and is dedicated to and for all we humans who seek to encourage ourselves and others.

# Contents

# The Positive Person's Proclamation

This is going to be a great day!

For I am going to picture in my mind

the positive outcome of a predetermined plan!


And I am going to be so committed to a positive

purpose, that it will propel me with power

and propensity to the very peak of my potential!


I was born to succeed!

I will succeed!

I am succeeding!

Today is my moment and now is my story!

# What Is Success?

It's being your best!
It's conceiving a plan,
It's believing you can!
It's giving your all,
It's getting up when you fall.
It's going the extra mile,
still wearing a positive smile.
It's growing each day
by study, work, and play.
What is success?
It's being your best!

# Mountain Top or Valley?

It's not on the mountain top, but in the valleys
that all that's great within us rallies.
We look for ease, but does it really please?
Isn't it when we're put to the test that we're
really at our best?
It's the storm that makes the eagle rise,
It's by solving problems you receive the prize.
See where your true fulfillment lies—
It's right before your eyes.
It's not on the mountain TOP,
but in the valleys that all
that's great within us rallies!

# The Winning Edge

My personal best is the real test,

It's the winning edge

It's Victory's Pledge, to all I can be.

It's not only victory for me, but victory for thee.

My personal best is the real test

that I've totally invested, all I've ingested.

It's giving my all getting up when I fall.

We walk this way but once,

So let's give it our best punch!

My personal best is really the test.

It's the Winning Edge.

It's Victory's Pledge!

# He Can Who Thinks He Can!

It's not what you've done before that determines
if you fall or if you'll soar.
Hey! it's a brand new day—simply say,
"He can who thinks he can!"

How do you know what heights you may reach
what hidden powers life may teach?
Hey! It's a brand new day simply say:
"He can who thinks he can!"

The only limits to our pace, upon ourselves
we have placed.
Hey! It's a brand new day—simply say,
"He can who thinks he can!"

The greatness that we seek won't go to the doubter
or the meek, but to him who can say,

"He can who thinks he can!"

# Chart Your Course

O' Friend chart your course, and capture the
force that will make your journey full of purpose
and joy.
For the time that is now may be just like the flowers,
blooming today and tomorrow withering away.
Set goals that will challenge the best that's within—
Pulling us forward, helping us win.
O' Friend chart your course, for the greatest remorse is
to leave this course—never knowing
how great was your force!

# Tis the Bold That Get the Gold

Aye Maties, 'tis the bold that get the gold.
If ya sit back and wait you'll be left
Hanging at the gate.
For 'tis the bold that get the gold.
If you never take a chance it's a cinch
You won't advance.
For 'tis the bold that get the gold.
'Tis true opportunity all around us knocks.
But it's up to us to break the mental locks.
For 'tis the bold that get the gold.
Many tales have been told about a man's
Elusive search for gold,
But they'll all be losers in the cold,
Until they grasp the truth—
'Tis the bold that get the Gold!

# He Never Tried

He could have been a ship builder,
almost any profession was within his stride,
But he never tried.

He could have scaled the mountains high,
or sailed the whole world wide,
But he never tried.

Some say it was because of or the lack of pride,
But he never tried.

Great songs unsung, so many things undone,
remain inside,
Because he never tried.

The joys that were missed, the friends eclipsed,
Because he never tried.

When opportunity had past (passed), and he's about
to breath his last, he broke down and bitterly cried,
Because he'd never really tried.

# Don't Wait to Be Told

Don't wait to be told, step up and grab hold,
the job will never get done, if you've
never begun.
Don't wait to be told, or you'll be left out in
the cold
See what needs to be done, and send
problems on the run.

Don't wait to be told, to the bold
goes the gold!
Calls to be made—Products Displayed.
Don't wait to be told when so many
are waiting to be sold.

So don't wait to be told, break the lethargic
mold, and watch victory unfold!
Don't wait to be told.

# What Is Desire

What is desire?
It's not just a wish,
It's a raging fire, that builds and inspires us,
lifting us higher.

What is desire?
It's not just a dream; it is a cascading stream,
that carries us on to the fulfillment of our dreams.

What is desire?
It is deciding what you want and wanting it more,
so that all that would distract you totally ignore.

It's not pie in the sky, but singleness of eye.
It's knowing where you're going, not talking,
but showing.

What is desire?
It's not just a wish but a raging fire that builds
and inspires us, lifting us higher!

# Ask and You Shall Receive

If you ask you're going to receive,

the reward will be greater than you can believe.

If you seek you're going to find the results

will boggle your mind.

If you knock the door will open,

all barriers will be broken,

total success will be your token.

# Thoughts

Thought is a cause that affects our life.
It can bring us joy or bring us strife.
It can make us a bore, or excite us to explore.
It can lead us to the top, or make us a flop.
The thoughts that we choose,
will cause us to win or to lose.

Thought is a cause, so pause—
you're about to cause the affects
that will decide a life of regret or of pride.
YOU DECIDE!

# What Keeps Me from Being All I Can Be?

What keeps me from being all I can be?
What traitors are keeping total victory
from me.
The first is self-doubt; let's us turn it about,
Replace it with faith in your ability to win.
Next, knock fear on the chin, just face it
with a grin.
The biggest culprit of all, seeking to bring
our downfall,
Is just to sit on our rear, and not get in gear.
What keeps me from being all that I can be?
Not living up to the best that's within me!

# Begin

Only begin, that's the immediate thing.

I'll do it tomorrow is only to borrow more
sorrow.

Only begin and you've started to win.

The people who put you off, will only incur
scoff.

Only begin, that's the immediate thing.

It's easy to delay, to fool around and play.

Only begin, that's the immediate thing.

You can't change yourself by staying on the
shelf.

Only begin, that's the immediate thing,

The real fun is not when it's done, but when
you've really begun.

There is only one sin and that's not to begin.

So get out of your rut, spread your feathers
and strut.

Only begin, that's the immediate thing!

# Staying Up

How do you keep your spirits up,
When everything seems to go wrong, the day
seems so long, problems prolonged?

How do you keep your spirits up,
When nothing seems to go right, every dollar
you have seems to take flight?

How do you keep your spirits up?
Just give up?
NO!

It's not what happens to you or me, but what we
perceive it to be.
That's the real key.

Look for the best when you're put to the test,
and never give up!
That is how you keep your spirits up!

# Be the Best Me

What others may be, doesn't add or detract
from me,
I must be the best I can be.
There are others that are richer and some are
poorer,
Some are taller, some are smaller.
But what others may be, what's it to me?
I must be, the best I can be!

# What If?

What if I'd made that extra call?

What if I'd continued when I was in a stall?

What a difference it might have made if I'd
gone instead of stayed?

What if I'd offered a helping hand, instead of
burying my head in the sand?

What if I'd set a higher goal, kept going when
I hit a troubled shoal?

What if I read a little every day, instead of
whiling the time away?

What if I really gave life my all, pushed through
all limiting walls?

What if?

# Within Me

There's a whole lot of me no one can see, not even me.
I really want to be, all I can be.
But so much is still hidden within me.

I made earnest pleas to set these talents free,
as thought someone else possessed the key.
What a surprise to see,
all along the answers were within me.

# Grace under Pressure

They say that grace under pressure
is the price of success.
Easy to profess, tougher to possess,
so many demands, conflicting commands.

How can you hang loose
when you feel shot at like a goose,
hunted like a moose?
The secret is to say: Hey! Who's in command?
I'm the leader of this band and the band is me!

The music that is played and on my mind displayed,
Is a matter of my choice, not some other's voice.
Grace under pressure, the price of success,
Hey, it's within me! Even God would agree!

## It's Up to Me

If it's going to be, it's up to me!
I'll be no further tomorrow than I am today,
unless I'm prepared to pay my own way.
It's so easy to plea, it's not up to me,
My misfortune or pain, or some others
I'll blame.
But if I'm to gain any real acclaim, to win
at this game,
I must light my own flame, because if it's
going to be,
It's really up to me!

# Aloha

Aloha. Aloha! What a strange word.

It means hello, and it means goodbye.
Whether you're heading out or returning, via
sea or by sky, why not say aloha, goodbye,
to ways that lead nowhere, and say aloha,
hello, to ways that lead somewhere.

Say aloha, goodbye, to that which is less
than your best. Say aloha, hello, to that
which puts pride in your chest. Say aloha,
goodbye, to hate and to fear; say aloha,
hello, to love and good cheer.

Say aloha, hello, to all that's positive in life.
Say aloha, goodbye, to all negation and strife.
Aloha, aloha, what a strange word.
It means hello and it means goodbye.

# Stress

How can we best handle anxiety and stress?
It's so easy to get riled, to reguile, and be vile.
Put this simple truth to the test:

It always works best!
Take time to respond, it's like waving a wand.
Picture your mind as still as a pond.
Want to avoid a lot of stress and strife?
Refuse to let others take charge of your life.

How can we best handle anxiety and stress?
Quit putting yourself down and recognize your best!

How can we best handle anxiety and stress?
Recognize friend, it lies in your breast!

# Worry!

Worry, worry, you cause such a fury.
You're about to waste my time.

With the time I spend with you,
I think of all the great things
I'd rather do.

So worry, worry, I'm giving you the gate,
Productive time is my new mate.

# Celebrate Yourself

Celebrate yourself, you're one of a kind.

You're a gift from above, a person to love!

Celebrate yourself!

Be your best friend from beginning to end.

Celebrate yourself!

Be all you can be then you will see

the celebration is for thee!

Celebrate yourself!

# Truth

If it is the truth that sets us free,

what does untruth have to do with me?

Would I choose chains,

instead of all that freedom gains?

O' Friend spare yourself the pain,

In your life let truth and freedom rein.

# Do It Now!

Turn your talk, into your walk.

Do it now!

Put your hand to the plow and show them how.

Do it now!

Got some task undone, some victory to be won?

Do it now!

Calls to make, cakes to bake.

Do it now!

The sun will set, you'll soon forget, so:

Do it now!

# You Were Born To Win!

Lift up your chin, face life with a grin,

You were born to win!

Don't say that others get breaks,

you haven't what it takes,

You were born to win!

Sure you've had some tough times,

been down to your last dime,

But there is still plenty of time,

You were born to win!

Take time to reflect, give others respect,

You were born to win!

Make the best use of your time.

It's the key to your climb,

You were born to win!

Set goals, surmount shoals,

it's for you the bell tolls!

You were born to win!

# A Solution for Sorrow

Is there any simple solution for sorrow?

Some magic potion I can borrow?

Grief has robbed my peace like a vagrant thief.

O' the loneliness within, the ache in my heart,

a feeling as though a part of me had died.

Has our Master lied? When His promise He cried?

"Blessed are they that morn,

for they shall be comforted."

I think not!

The solution I'm sure is to rest in Him secure,

the agony will cease.

He will bring you His peace!

# If I Could Redesign the World

If I could redesign the world: I'd seek to eliminate
all pain, no hurt or sorrow would remain. The only
tears would be tears of joy. Total fulfillment would
be everyone's employ. The lame would walk, the
dumb would talk, the blind would see.

If I could redesign the world, there would be no war,
only peace forever more.

The pangs of loneliness would flee, in its place a
sense of glee. But, wait, if I redesign the world with-
out pain, what warning sign would yet remain? And
if there were no tears of sorrow, would I be fit to
serve tomorrow?

If total fulfillment was had by each, where is the
need to stretch and reach? If the lame could walk, the
dumb talk, the blind see, where is the need of a
healing ministry?
If war was to cease, where is the need for those who
lead us to peace? If loneliness were to flee a comfort-
ing friend need not be.

If I could redesign the world? NO! It's clear. It was
Designed just for what we see, which is really best for
you and me!

# It's Never Too Late!

You say it's too late. You're a victim of fate.
It's never too late, just get going don't wait!
There are jobs to be done, songs to be sung.
It's never too late!

You say you're too old, you're ready to fold,
Hey, it's never too late.

Each day is a clean slate, new things to learn,
places to go, so get on with the show!
It's never too late.

Break out of the gate, step up to the plate.
Each new day will prove it's just great to realize,
It's never too late!

# The Best Is Yet to Come

If you think you've seen the best,
brethren wait until you see the rest!
The best is yet to come!

You've crossed over many boulders,
but now you're standing on your shoulders,
The best in yet to come!

You think you've had some fun,
but it's really only begun!
The best is yet to come!

You think you've seen and felt it all,
but brother the future will be a royal ball,
The best is yet to come!

Forget the past even though it was a blast,
The best is yet to come!
So hang on to hope, grab the rope, learn to cope.
The best is yet to come!

# Chariots or Chuckholes

Chariots or chuckholes which will it be?
The ultimate answer is up to me. My attitude toward the
problem I face, will life me like a chariot on the race or drop
me in a chuckhole out of the race.

There's no promise that life will always be a breeze, no
problems or trouble just lots of ease. Hey, life can be mean
and cause you to scream, but it's the problems that test and bring
out our best.

It's our positive response to the things that seem rough, that builds
us up! Making us winning tough! Chariots or chuckholes which
will it be? The ultimate answer is up to me.

My attitude toward the problem I face will lift me like a chariot
on with the race or drop me in a chuckhole out to the race.

# An Extra Miler

Are you an "Extra Miler" or just an
"Enough to Get by-er?"
Do you set goals that fill you with desire,
or just give it a try until you tire?
Brother, being an "Extra Miler" will give you real fire!
You'll leave the "Just Enough To Get By-er"
smoldering in his mire.
Do you always give your best?
Or just what's expected and let others do the rest?
If you've been a "Just Enough To Get By-er"
why not set your sights a little higher become
an "Extra Miler!"

# The Pictures in Our Mind

It's the pictures we hold in our mind that
will determine if it's failure or success
we will find.

Hold a picture of the person you would like to be,
until that's the person you eventually see.

Picture yourself achieving your goals,
overcoming and surmounting life's
toughest shoals.

For it's the pictures we hold in our mind that will
determine if it's failure or success we will find.

What blinds us from beholding the benefits that
are before us?

Are we standing so close to the trees that we miss
the forest?

Grant that the scales may fall from our eyes that
we might behold all the bounty and benefits that
before us lies.

For it's the pictures we hold in our mind that will
determine if it's failure or success we will find.

# Faith

What is faith? It's occupying new territory.
It's seeking new horizons. It's stretching and reaching
beyond familiar ground.

Faith is for the upward and outward bound.
It is not seeing, it is just believing there's a better way,
causing and influencing our every sway.

What is faith? It's acting on ideas, expecting the best, not
giving up when we're put to the test. It's putting our life on
the line, going for broke each and every time, for faith is
the force that makes victory our course.

What is faith? It's occupying new territory.
It's seeking new horizons. It's stretching and reaching
beyond familiar ground.
Faith is for the upward and outward bound!

# The Affirmative Person's Affirmation

Think success!

We become what we think about!

He can who thinks he can!

Visualize, then actualize!

Attitude determines our altitude!

Encourage excellence in everyone!

Success is the progressive realization

of a worthy ideal or goal!

Make a positive difference

wherever you are!

Do it now!

# About the Author

At the age of sixteen Jim Bernard crossed the Columbia River Bar as an ordinary seaman. He received his Deck Officer's license at twenty-one and served during the Korean War.

In college, Jim majored in business, psychology, and religion.

After leaving the sea Jim went on to build an insurance and real estate business in Portland, Oregon. After selling the business, Jim and Cherie moved to Astoria, Oregon where Jim assisted in the management of a Ford dealership.

Jim and Cherie charter fished out of Hammond, Oregon. Jim, until recently, served as a captain and guide at Yes Bay, Alaska taking guests fishing for salmon, halibut and other bottom fish.

Jim served as an elder and teaches in the Presbyterian Church.

Jim and Cherie live in Warrenton, Oregon, less than a mile from the Mighty Columbia River. They are proud parents of four children, fourteen grandchildren, and twenty great-grandchildren. They have been happily married for sixty-six years and have always been blessed by a living and loving Lord.

# Books by the Author

Alaska Fishing Adventures (2015)

Inspirational Nautical Poems and Prose (2015)

Making the Principles of Success a Habit

Positive Poems and Rhymes (2015)

Positive Thoughts for a Profitable Day (2015)

The Adventures of a Young Merchant Sailor (2015)

Made in the
USA
Monee, IL

15841978R00026